D0295525

Aberdeenshire
C O U N C I L

Aberdeenshire Libraries
www.aberdeenshire.gov.uk/libraries
Renewals Hotline 01224 661511

3 1 NOV 2017

2 3 JUN 2018

Gray, Leon

ABERDEENSHIRE
LIBRARY &
INFORMATION SERVICES

WITHDRAWN
FROM LIB

Aberdeenshire

3155034

ABERDEENSHIRE LIBRARIES	
3155034	
Bertrams	05/01/2015
J577.64	£12.99

Amazing Habitats

RIVERS AND LAKES

W

FRANKLIN WATTS
LONDON•SYDNEY

This edition first published in 2015
by Franklin Watts
338 Euston Road
London NW1 3BH

Franklin Watts Australia
Level 17/207 Kent Street
Sydney, NSW 2000

Copyright © 2014
Brown Bear Books Ltd

All rights reserved. No part of this publication
may be reproduced, stored in a retrieval
system, or transmitted in any form or by any
means, electronic, mechanical, photocopying,
recording or otherwise, without the prior
written permission of the copyright owner.

A CIP catalogue record for this book
is available from the British Library.

ISBN: 978-1-4451-3205-1

Dewey no. 577.6'4

Printed in China

Franklin Watts is a division of
Hachette Children's Books,
an Hachette UK company.
www.hachette.co.uk

Note to parents and teachers concerning
websites: In the book every effort has been
made by the Publishers to ensure that
websites are suitable for children, that they
are of the highest educational value, and that
they contain no inappropriate or offensive
material. However, because of the nature of
the Internet, it is impossible to guarantee that
the contents of these sites will not be altered.
We advise that Internet access is supervised
by a responsible adult.

Author: Leon Gray
Designer: Karen Perry
Picture Researcher: Clare Newman
Editor: Tim Harris
Children's Publisher: Anne O'Daly
Design Manager: Keith Davis
Editorial Director: Lindsey Lowe

Picture Credits

The photographs in this book are used by
permission and through the courtesy of:

Cover main, ©Mike Lane/FLPA; cover background,
©Shutterstock; 1, ©Nattanan726/Shutterstock;
2-3, ©Dmitry Naumov/Shutterstock; 4-5, ©RIRF
Stock/Shutterstock; 5cr, ©Tony Campbell/
Shutterstock; 6cl, ©Bebay/Shutterstock; 6bl,
©Anton Ivanoc/Shutterstock; 6bc, ©Matthew
Dixon/Shutterstock; 7tr, ©Mikhail Markovsky/
Shutterstock; 7cr, ©Fritz 16/Shutterstock;
7bl, ©Przemyslaw Skibiriski/Shutterstock; 8-9,
©Frank11/Shutterstock; 9cr, ©Tomaz Kunst/
Shutterstock; 10, ©Alice Nerr/Shutterstock;
11c, ©Max Mindenthaler/Shutterstock; 11br,
©Mickolay Vinokirov/Shutterstock; 12, ©Luck
Luckyfarm/Shutterstock; 13, ©rdonar/Shutterstock;
14, ©Wildnedpix/Shutterstock; 15, ©Wikipedia;
16, ©HTU/Shutterstock; 17, ©John Carnemo Ila/
Dreamstime; 18bl, ©Kim Taylor/Nature PL/Corbis;
19tr, ©Hamsterman/Shutterstock; 19, ©Ongm/
Dreamstime; 20, ©Andre Anita/Shutterstock; 21tr,
©Petr Podrouzek/Shutterstock; 21br, ©Ignacia
Sulavena/Shutterstock; 22-23, ©Nattanan726/
Shutterstock; 23cr, ©De Visu/Shutterstock; 24,
©Pete Spiro/Shutterstock; 24t, ©Ivan Sazykin/
Shutterstock; 25br, ©Aneese/iStock/Thinkstock;
26-27, ©gopixgo/Shutterstock; 27tr, ©Christian
Draghici/Shutterstock; 28cl, ©Mickolay Vinokirov/
Shutterstock; 28cr, ©Mickolay Vinokirov/
Shutterstock; 28b ©Ongm/Dreamstime; 29c,
©Luck Luckyfarm/Shutterstock; 29b, ©De Visu/
Shutterstock.

t=top, c=centre, b=bottom, l=left, r=right

Brown Bear Books has made every attempt
to contact the copyright holder. If you have
any information please contact
licensing@brownbearbooks.co.uk

CONTENTS

• • • • • • • • • • • • • • ➤

INTRODUCTION

Water is one of the reasons that life on Earth is possible. Rivers and lakes are important **sources** of water. These watery habitats are home to many different animals and plants. We also rely on rivers for fresh drinking water and water to help crops grow.

A bald eagle plucks a salmon from Lake Chilkat, Alaska, in the USA.

Habitats are places where animals or plants live and grow. Some animals and plants live in grasslands or dry deserts. Some live in, on or beside rivers and lakes. Rivers are channels of fresh water that wind across the land. Most begin high up in hills and mountains and flow down to the sea. Lakes and ponds are pools of water that fill hollow **basins** in the land. Some stretches of water, such as giant inland seas, contain salty water.

Read on to find out what rivers and lakes are like – and how plants, animals and people live in, on and around them.

HIGH POINT

Snake River, Idaho, in the USA, starts life as tiny mountain streams. As water flows down the slopes, the streams join to form the giant winding river.

5

WORLD RIVERS AND

Rivers and lakes are found all over the world.
This map shows some of the major rivers and
lakes to be found on the world's continents.

The city of Chicago is
built on the shore of
Lake Michigan in the USA.

NORTH
AMERICA

SOUTH
AMERICA

The city of London
in England is built
along the banks o⸗
the River Thames.

The River Amazon flows
through the Amazon rainforest
in South America. It is 6,400
km (4,000 miles) long.

ANTARCTICA

LAKES

Rivers and
Lakes

Lake Baikal in
Russia contains
20 per cent
of the world's
supply of
fresh water.

EUROPE

ASIA

AFRICA

AUSTRALIA

A paddle steamer
cruises along the
River Murray in
southern Australia.

A rainbow forms as water from
the River Zambezi, on the border
between Zambia and Zimbabwe in
Africa, spills over Victoria Falls.

CLIMATE

Rivers and lakes play a vital role in the **water cycle**, which helps shape the weather on our planet. They also have some of the most varied climates of all Earth's habitats.

LIFELINE

The Nile in Egypt, Africa, is the world's longest river. It carries water through the Sahara Desert, allowing crops to be grown along its banks.

Water is constantly recycled around our planet. It moves between air, land and the oceans. This movement is called the water cycle. Sunlight warms the water in rivers, lakes and oceans. This water **evaporates** and rises to form clouds. The clouds get bigger and heavier and eventually release water as rain or snow. Eventually most of it ends up back in the rivers and oceans.

Heavy rain clouds over Lake Victoria in Uganda, Africa.

Changing climate

Rivers and lakes are very different from place to place. In polar regions, the water in rivers and lakes freezes over for most of the year. In deserts, it can be so hot that the water evaporates. Rivers and lakes dry up and disappear. Some rivers regularly flood the surrounding land. This can destroy habitats and the homes of people who live there. Rivers also shape the land. The flowing water grinds away the rock, carving **valleys** in the landscape. The river then carries the **sediment** down to the sea, where it is released.

BIO FACT
Angel Falls in Venezuela, South America, is the world's tallest waterfall at 979 metres (3,212 feet). Clouds form above the forests on the tepuis (table-top) mountain. The rain then feeds the waterfall.

Tepuis mountain

WOW!

• Lake Eyre in Australia lies in a desert and is usually almost dry. If heavy rain falls in mountains far to the north, rivers carry water into the lake. When it is full, the lake is 6 metres (20 feet) deep.

It is easier to travel by snowmobile when the River Mackenzie freezes over during the Canadian winter.

Dead Sea

The Dead Sea is a salt lake on the border of Israel and Jordan in the Middle East. Water flows into the Dead Sea from rivers and streams, but no water flows out. This water dissolves rocks at the bottom of the lake. The Sun then evaporates the water, making the lake very salty. In fact, it is so salty that no animals and plants can live there.

PLANTS

Many different plants depend on rivers and lakes for their survival. Some live in the water, while others cling to rocks or grow on the river banks.

The most common plants found in rivers and lakes are so small you need a **microscope** to see them. They are called **algae** and they are not true plants. These tiny **organisms** do not have roots, stems and leaves. Algae make food in the same way as plants, using energy from the Sun. In turn, algae are food for many of the animals that live in rivers and lakes.

Water lilies

Plants called water lilies live in the deeper parts of some ponds and lakes. Their waxy leaves and colourful flowers float on the surface of the water. The stems grow up from the bed of the lake or pond towards the sunlight.

ON THE ROCKS

Simple plants called mosses and liverworts grow on rocks in rivers. The roots cling tightly onto the surface of the rocks so the plants are not swept away by the water current.

BIO FACT

Lake Natron in Tanzania, Africa, is too salty to support plant growth. Instead, tiny salt–loving organisms live in the water. They give the lake its deep red colour.

Amazon floods

During the rainy season, the River Amazon bursts its banks. Water floods the surrounding forest to form lagoons. This flooding is an important process. The water returns important **nutrients** to the soil. When the floodwater levels subside, new plants take root and renew the rainforest.

Water weeds

Many plants thrive in the nutrient-rich waters of rivers and lakes. In fact some plants, such as duckweed and water hyacinth, grow so well people view them as **weeds**. These plants grow very quickly and the leaves spread out to cover the surface of the water. They crowd out other plants that grow in the water. Eventually, the dense carpet of vegetation stops oxygen from reaching the water below, which can suffocate the animals that live underwater.

Water crowfoot is a common water weed found in the rivers of North America and Europe.

ANIMALS

Numerous types of animals live in or near rivers and lakes. Some spend all of their lives in water. Others grow up in water but leave when they become adults. Many simply visit to feed or drink.

GONE FISHING

A kingfisher plucks a fish from the surface of a lake. These birds have sharp, pointy beaks to spear their slippery **prey.**

More than one-third of the world's 25,000 fish species live in freshwater rivers and lakes. Many insect **larvae** (young) develop in water and leave when they become adults. **Amphibians**, such as frogs, follow a similar life cycle.

Many other animals use rivers and lakes as hunting grounds. Birds such as bald eagles and ospreys swoop down to catch fish from the water's surface. **Mammals**, such as otters and voles, hunt in rivers and live in burrows in the river banks.

Rudder-like tail

Shape of bill is same as a duck's bill

Webbed feet

Sharp claws

Duck-billed platypus

The duck-billed platypus lives in rivers and creeks in Australia. This unusual mammal is well-adapted to life in the water. It has sleek waterproof fur, a broad tail and webbed feet, which help it to swim quickly. Unlike most other mammals, the platypus lays eggs instead of giving birth to live young. She raises them in a tunnel in the river bank.

Fishy food chain

Fish are perfectly adapted to life in rivers and lakes. With their streamlined shape, scaly bodies and powerful fins, many different fish thrive in these watery habitats. These animals are an important link in the **food chains** of rivers and lakes. Fish eat a wide range of food. Some feed on microscopic algae, trapping the tiny organisms on their **gills**. Most eat other animals, such as insects and other fish. In turn, fish provide food for many other animals, such as otters and seals.

SEAL LIFE

Baikal seals (right) live in the landlocked waters of Lake Baikal in Siberia, Russia. They are the only seals to spend all their lives in fresh water.

Waterproof fur

A young brown trout leaps from the surface of the water to catch a passing damselfly.

Feeding frenzy

The red-bellied piranha is one of the most fearsome **predators** of the Amazon. These meat-eating fish swim in shoals in the rivers that flow through the rainforest. The piranhas are mainly **scavengers** but sometimes go into a 'feeding frenzy,' using their sharp teeth to rip apart prey, such as other fish.

Nostrils close when underwater

A third eyelid covers each eye

Sharp claws

Water predators

Strong swimmers, such as otters, and **reptiles**, including alligators and crocodiles, are deadly predators in rivers and lakes. The grizzly bear is another predator that hunts in some rivers in North America. Every year, wild salmon return from the oceans to lay their eggs in rivers. The bears pluck the salmon from the water as they swim upstream against the current.

A grizzly bear catches a salmon. The bears feast on salmon returning to rivers to lay their eggs.

RIVER KILLER

Dragonflies are deadly predators. The young **nymphs** live in water and snatch passing prey. The winged adults catch other flying insects in mid-air.

Crocodile attack

Crocodiles are predators that hunt in warm, tropical river and lake habitats. These reptiles are **carnivores** and will eat anything they can catch, from fish to small mammals. Large crocodiles regularly attack people. They are very quick and strike before their prey can react.

PEOPLE

People have always relied on rivers and lakes for survival. We use the fresh water to drink and to clean our bodies and our clothes. Today, many people enjoy river sports such as canoeing and rafting.

In developing countries, people still fish rivers and lakes for food and hunt the animals that live near them. In fact, many modern cities have developed from the small villages people built along rivers and lakes. Some rivers and lakes are so important that many people consider them to be **sacred** places. The River Ganges in India is sacred to many people.

Farmers also rely on rivers and lakes. A river's natural cycle of flooding adds nutrients to the soil, making it easier for farmers to grow crops. Rivers and lakes also provide water for the crops. This is called **irrigation**.

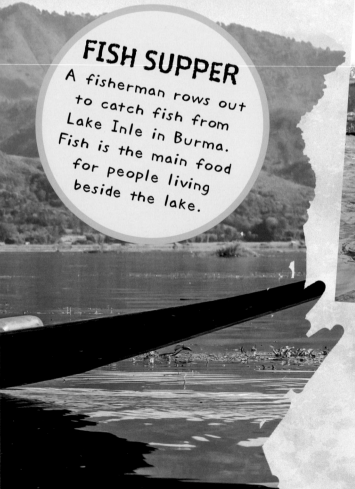

FISH SUPPER

A fisherman rows out to catch fish from Lake Inle in Burma. Fish is the main food for people living beside the lake.

Hindus bathe in the River Ganges. The river is sacred to them.

On the move

Before the age of motor transport, people often relied on rivers to move around. They could transport themselves and their goods much more easily than walking across the land. The first boats were made by tying logs together with strong reeds. Later, people hollowed out logs to make canoes and propelled them through the water using oars. Eventually, people harnessed the power of the wind and built huge sailing ships. Explorers sailed across the oceans in these ships to discover new lands.

CANAL FACTS

In many parts of the world, people have built canals to transport people and their belongings. The Panama Canal is the world's longest canal. It links the Pacific and Atlantic oceans in Central America.

Yachts crowd a marina on Lake Michigan on the Chicago waterfront. Sailing is a popular hobby for many people.

Thrill-seekers take part in a white-water rafting race on the River Belaya in Russia.

River cruise

A paddle steamer takes tourists on a cruise down the Mississippi River in the USA. These boats were once used to transport people and goods along rivers. The steam engines have been replaced with modern diesel engines.

THE FUTURE

Rivers and lakes are some of our most varied and beautiful habitats, but their future remains uncertain. Human activities are damaging them and the plants and animals that live in them.

One of the major causes for concern is **pollution**. Human activities, such as farming and industry, pollute rivers and lakes. The harmful chemicals from factories and farms run off the land and end up in rivers and lakes. As they build up in the water, the chemicals kill the animals and plants that live there.

Climate change is another problem for rivers and lakes. As Earth's temperature increases, the water in rivers and lakes dries up. Many countries are also building dams across rivers to generate electricity from the water. This disrupts the river's natural flow, which in turn harms the animals and plants that live further upstream.

Dead fish are a tell-tale sign of river pollution. Toxic chemicals build up in the bodies of the fish and kill them.

ARAL SEA

The Aral Sea was once a huge lake in central Asia. Rivers that flowed into it were blocked, so the lake has shrunk to a fraction of its former size.

QUIZ

Try this quiz to test your knowledge of rivers and lakes. You can find the answers on page 31.

1 Which European capital city is built along the banks of the River Thames?

2 The Dead Sea gets its name because no animals or plants can live there. Why?

3 These seals live in a landlocked lake in the middle of Siberia in Russia. What is the name of this lake?

4 What plant lives on the surface of some ponds and lakes and has these colourful flowers?

Fact File

- Most rivers start as small streams high in the mountains and flow down to the sea.

- Lakes form when water collects in basins in the land.

- Rivers are an important source of fresh water for animals, plants and people.

- Water moves between the air, land and sea in a journey called the water cycle.

- Human activities such as farming and dam building are destroying rivers and lakes.

5 The River Ganges in India is sacred to people from which religion?

Winners and losers

⬆ Otters have become more common in Britain's rivers. That is because many chemicals that harmed the otters in the past have now been banned.

⬇ There are now no river dolphins living in the Yangtze River in China. They died out because they got caught up in fishing nets or collided with boats.

GLOSSARY

algae: Tiny plant-like organisms that live in rivers and lakes.

amphibians: Animals, such as frogs, which start life in the water, but move onto the land as adults.

basin: A hollow in the surface of the land into which water drains to form a lake.

carnivores: Animals that only eat meat. Crocodiles are carnivores.

evaporate: To change from a liquid to a gas. Water from rivers and lakes evaporates to form clouds.

food chain: The order in which animals feed on plants and other animals within a habitat.

gills: The breathing organs of fish and other animals. The gills absorb oxygen, allowing animals to breathe underwater.

irrigation: When farmers use the water from rivers and lakes to water their crops.

larvae: The young form of animals such as insects and amphibians.

mammals: Animals with warm blood that breathe air using lungs. Mammals feed their young on milk.

microscope: An instrument that people use to see extremely small objects such as algae.

nutrients: Substances that provide food for growth.

nymphs: The young of some kinds of insects, before they change to their adult form.

organisms: A scientific word to describe any living thing, such as an animal or plant.

pollution: Dumping harmful chemicals into the environment.

predators: Animals that hunt and eat other animals.

prey: Animals that are hunted and eaten by other animals.

reptiles: Animals that usually have scaly skin and lay eggs. Crocodiles, snakes and turtles are reptiles.

sacred: Considered to be holy.

scavengers: Animals that feed on the remains of dead animals.

sediment: Fine material, such as mud and sand, carried by rivers.

sources: Places where something comes from.

species: A group of animals that look alike. Members of the same species can mate and produce young together.

valleys: A deep groove cut into the land by the force of flowing water.

water cycle: The journey that water takes as its moves between the air, land and the oceans.

weeds: Plants that crowd out cultivated plants.

FURTHER RESOURCES

Books

Gray. Leon. *Geographywise: Rivers*. Wayland (2010).

Green. Jen. *Rivers Around the World*. PowerKids Press (2009).

Harrison. Paul. *Journey Along a River* (series). Wayland (2012–2013).

Hewitt. Sally. *Project Geography: Rivers*. Franklin Watts (2012).

Johnson. Jinny. *Watery Worlds: Rivers and Lakes*. Franklin Watts (2012).

Manning. Paul. *River Adventures* (series). Franklin Watts.

Websites

BBC Nature. This site is a fantastic source of information about rivers and lakes. Click on the links under freshwater habitats to see stunning photos and videos along with links to information about the animals and plants that live in rivers and lakes. **www.bbc.co.uk/nature/habitats/**

National Geographic. Learn all about the world's freshwater habitats. Find out what you can do help protect these fragile habitats. Includes stunning photographs and videos. **www.kids.nationalgeographic. com/kids/activities/new/ocean/**

Primary Homework Help. A useful site packed with interesting and easy-to-understand text and diagrams about rivers. The site has many links to other helpful websites . **www.primaryhomeworkhelp.co. uk/rivers/websites**

World Wide Fund for Nature. Photos, videos, animals and plants that live in freshwater rivers and lakes. Read about some of the conservation plans for the world's freshwater habitats, and find out what you can do to help. **www.worldwildlife.org/habitats/ freshwaters**

Answers to the Quiz: 1 London. 2 Because the water is too salty. 3 Lake Baikal. 4 Water lily. 5 Hindu.

INDEX